DORIC LAYS AND LYRICS

BY

JAMES THOMSON

HAWICK

EDINBURGH

SETON & MACKENZIE 81 GEORGE STREET

MDCCCLXX

TO

HIS NUMEROUS SUBCRIBERS

THE AUTHOR

MOST RESPECTFULLY AND AFFECTIONATELY DEDICATES

THIS LITTLE VOLUME

IN TOKEN OF HIS GRATITUDE FOR THEIR KIND SUPPORT AND

ZEAL IN THE PROMOTION OF ITS SUCCESS.

PREFACE.

The Author of this Little Volume may state that most of the Pieces have from time to time appeared in the columns of Newspapers and Periodicals.

In presenting them in a collected form, he will offer no apology,—the Public being the best judges of their merits or demerits.

They are the production of his leisure hours in the occupation of a Journeyman Wood Turner,—and their composition has at least served to wile away many an irksome hour, and relieve the tedium of a monotonous existence.

Should any of these simple Rhymes be the means of touching a chord in the heart, or kindling a smile of happiness and enjoyment at the fireside of the Sons of Toil, the Author will be amply rewarded.

Hawick, *March* 1870.

CONTENTS.

DORIC LAYS AND LYRICS.

The Widow's Lament.

The last throe is o'er, and the last sigh is gi'en—
Smooth bye the grey hair,—close the glassy een.
Now take the Widow's blessin' for your kind heart and han',
And leave me alane wi' my Auld Guidman.

My tears they maun fa' when there's nae ane near;
My heart maun ha'e vent, and nae ane maun hear;
And I maun kiss the cauld lips again and again,
And pour out my sorrows o'er my Auld Guidman.

Mate o' my bosom for twa score o' years,

I gaze on thy form through the mist o' my tears ;

And the warld grows dark as thy closed een I scan,—

I had na'e friend on earth but my Auld Guidman.

The Bairnies are gane that I nursed on my knee,—

They were dear to my heart, they were fair to my e'e ;

I ha'e borne meikle sorrow in life's short span,

But the last blow's the warst ane—my Auld Guidman.

Gin this weary life was o'er, wi' its sorrow and its pain !

The last link is broken, the last tie is gane !

Oh to lie beside thee, were it Heaven's high plan,

And share the dreamless slumber o' my Auld Guidman.

There's a hope for the weary when the warld's hope is gane

There's rest in the grave for the friendless and lane ;

And a bright hame aboon in a far fairer lan',

Where I'll meet my bonny Bairnies and my Auld Guidman

Hairst.

"Robin shuire in hairst,
  I shuire wi' him;
Fient a huik I had,
  Yet I stack by him."

BURNS.

The yellow corn waves in the field,
  The merry hairst's begun;
And steel plate sickles, sharp and keen,
  Are glintin' in the sun.
While strappin' lads and lasses braw,
  A' kiltit to the knee,
Bring to my mind a hairst langsyne,
  When Robin shuire wi' me.

Light lie the mools upon his breast;
   He was a strappin' chield,—
A better shearer ne'er drew huik
   Upon a harvest field.
And didna joy loup in my heart,
   And sparkle frae my e'e,
Sae proud was I, when Robin said
   He'd shear along wi' me.

That was a lightsome hairst to me,—
   For love maks light o' toil,—
The kindly blink o' Robin's e'e
   Could a' my care beguile.
At restin' time amang the stooks
   I sat upon his knee,
And wondered if the warld could haud
   A blither lass than me.

Lang Sandy and his sister Jean
   Thocht nane wi' them could shear,
And a' the hairst at Rab an' me
   Threw mony a taunt an' jeer.

Rab ga'e them aye as guid's they brought,
 And took it a' in fun ;
But inly vowed to heat their skin
 Afore the hairst was dune.

The kirn day cam', a kemp began,
 And hard and fast it grew ;
Across the rig wi' lightnin' speed
 The glintin' sickles flew.
Lang Sandy wamlet like an eel,
 But soon fell in the rear ;
For no a pair in a' the boon
 Wi' Rab an' me could shear.

We cleared our rig baith tight and clean
 And thought the day our ain,
When, waes my heart, I brak my huik
 Upon a meikle stane.
'Mak bands," quo' Robin ; while the sweat
 Like rain-draps trickled down ;
But Robin reached the land end first
 And foremost o' the boon.

I thought that I wad swoon wi' joy
  When, dightin' Robin's brow,
He says, " Meg, gin ye'll buckle to',
  I'll shear through life wi you."
What could I do but buckle to?
  He was sae frank an' free ;—
And often did I bless the day
  That Robin shuire wi' me.

To a Child at Play.

———

Merry little Maiden
  Skipping at thy play,
Gladsome as the wild bee
  Singing all the day.
Happy as the song bird
  On the forest bough,
Tossing back the ringlets
  From thy sunny brow.

Beauty in thy dimples,
  Mirth within thine eye,
Like a burst of music
  Is thy joyous cry.

Gazing on thy beauty
    Care forgets its pain ;
List'ning to thy music
    Age grows young again.

Oh, if thou could'st ever be
    Beautiful as now !
No care upon thy bosom !
    No cloud upon thy brow !
May He who watcheth over youth,
    Keep thee undefiled !
Smoothing still thy path of life,
    Happy little child.

Our Robin.

—————

THE blasts o' the winter, sae bitter and keen,
Had reft the sward o' its brightest green ;
The flowers were gane frae the hill and lea,
And the brown leaf fa'en frae the sapless tree,—
When a wee bird left the cheerless glen
To seek the hames and the haunts o' men ;
And langin' look'd through the window pane
At our cosie bield and our warm hearthstane.

We took the weary wanderer in
Frae the snawy drift an' the wintry win' ;
A welcome blithe we gied the chield
To share the warmth o' our cosie bield.

He shook the frost frae his "chitterin' wing,"
Syne thow'd his taes, and began to sing;
And the bairnies clap'd their hands wi' glee
At his bosom red and his glintin' e'e.

As the wee bird sang his lo'esome strain
A dream o' my bairnhood cam' back again,—
A vision sweet o' happier hours,
O' sunny glens and leafy bowers;
A lowly cot 'neath a roof o' strae,
And a little band that ha'e passed away
Frae sunny glens where the blossoms hang,—
A' swep'd o'er my heart at the Robin's sang!

Hogmanay.

Up frae their cosy beds
  Afore the peep o' day,
Skippin' round the corner,
  Brattlin' down the brae ;
Hearts a' sae happy,
  Faces blithe and gay,
A merry band o' bairnies
  Seek their Hogmanay.

Careless o' the blast sae bleak,
  Snawy drift or shower,
Though the roses on their cheek
  Turn like the blaewart flower.

Frae ilka door they're jinkin'
　To hail the happy day;
And they a' gang a' linkin'
　To seek their Hogmanay.

Bonny bairnies come awa',
　It's little I've to gi'e,
But ye shall ha'e my blessin' a'
　An' ae bawbee.
When manhood's care comes o'er ye,
　Ye'll mind the merry day
When happy hearted bairnies
　Ye sought your Hogmanay.

March.

Young March thou wert ever a froward boy,
Storming in passion, laughing in joy;
Changing thy mood like a wayward thing,
Tasting of Winter, telling of Spring.

Thou hast brought no flowers for the honey bee,
No glad green leaves for the forest tree,—
Save some little blossom that peeps from the spray
To mark if old Winter yet holds his sway.

Too soon, like the Dove, thou hast left thy ark,
The tempest lowers and the sky is dark;
Winter yet reigns with his icy cold,
Thou wilt die little bud ere thy leaves unfold.

An emblem art thou of life's fairest forms,
Opening their bloom to the world's cold storms,—
Fading away in adversity's breath,
Teaching a lesson of life and death !

Yet March thou art weaving rich vestures unseen,
Garlands of crimson, of yellow and green
And thy skies at times wear a brighter hue
To tell of the Summer's cloudless blue.

And thy sister will come, with her smile so sweet,
The dew on her robe, and the flowers at her feet,
Scattering her blossoms o'er mountain and plain,
Flushing the earth with her beauty again.

Time's Changes.

And can ye be the bonny lass
   That set the trysts wi' me !
And sat beside me on the grass
   'Aneath the hawthorn tree !
Is this the wee white hand,—the same
   That lay sae saft in mine !
Oh say, gin ye be Jeanie Grahame
   I lo'ed sae weel langsyne ?

Turn backward Carle Time wi' me
   Through twice ten years o' gloom,
And tak' me to the trystin' tree
   Amang the yellow broom.

And let me see the face sae fair,
  Sae innocent and young,
And listen to the tones ance mair,
  Like music frae her tongue.

You're sairly altered now, Jean,
  You're sairly altered now;
The spark o' light has left your e'en,
  The gloss is off your brow.
I've started frae my dreams by night,
  Your name upon my tongue;
But aye the vision met my sight
  Was beautiful and young!

But I forget the langsome years
  That o'er our head ha'e fled,
I didna' see the burning tears
  Thae e'en o' blue ha'e shed.
They tell o' meikle care and pain,
  They tell o' mony waes;
We needna' think to light again
  The love o' early days!

We canna bring auld feelings back,
   Our day o' love has gane ;
I still maun keep my onward track
   Unloved, and a' my lane.
Yet we may weel be friends at heart ;
   Though friendship's name is cauld ;-
O' Jeanie, wherefore did we pairt,
   Or why ha'e we grown auld ?

May.

Welcome smiling May,
  Thou darling of the year,
With all thy blossom gay
  The drooping heart to cheer.
Buds of beauty rare
  Meet the 'raptured eye,
Bursting everywhere
  Beneath the sunny sky.

In the sunlit dell
  Silvery waters glide,
Peace and Beauty dwell,
  Like sisters, side by side.

Merry little streams
   Dancing on their way,
Laughing 'neath thy beams
   Like a child at play.

Flowery bosom'd May,
   I loved thee when a boy,
Roaming all the day
   Daisied fields in joy.
Still thou hast the power,
   Nursling of the wild !
A spell in every flower,
   To melt me like a child.

Where dewy blossoms spring,
   Glist'ning in the Sun,
Where the wild birds sing,
   Each song a happy one.
There the knee will bend
   Upon the flowery sod,
And a prayer ascend
   Unto creation's God.

Eppy M'Gee.

She's a douse kind o' body, auld Eppy M'Gee,
A crouse kind o' body, auld Eppy M'Gee;
Though the waur o' the wear, she's as brisk as a bee,
And sound at the core yet, auld Eppy M'Gee.

She's wrestled wi' poortith, she's foughten wi' care,
And eydently toiled through the foul and the fair;
The heart scauds and sorrows that poortith maun dre
Couldna daunton the blithe heart o' Eppy M'Gee.

Lang fashed wi' a thriftless and drouthy guidman—
Wad ha'e drucken the ocean when ance he began;
But death stopped his whistle, and steekit his e'e,
' I'll ne'er tak' another," quo' Eppy M'Gee.

Left a widow—she brought up a family o' ten
To braw strappin' lasses and big buirdly men;
And ne'er frae the parish e'er sought a bawbee,—
She's a wonderfu' bodie, auld Eppie M'Gee.

Respec'it and liket by grit and by sma',
Wi' a couthie bit smile, and a kind word to a',
The puir beggar bodies o' lowly degree
A' bless the kind heart o' auld Eppy M'Gee.

The youngsters convene at her cosy fireside,
Where she sits like a queen in her glory and pride;
Syne wi' cootlin' and coakin', sae pauky and slee,
They get some queer story frae Eppy M'Gee.

O' pithy auld proverbs her mind is a mint,
She sings them queer ballants that ne'er were in print,
And syne gars them laugh till the tears fill their e'e—
Sic a droll kind o' bodie is Eppie M'Gee.

May guid aye befriend ye, auld Eppy M'Gee;
And blessings attend ye, auld Eppy M'Gee;
May care never dim the blythe blink o' your e'e,
Nor cloud your kind heart, couthie Eppy M'Gee.

Cousin Tom.

Dear Tom, I've now a little time,
   Which I'll devote to thee,
In stringing up a bit o' rhyme
   To send across the sea.
And could I hope this simple lay
   Had power to win thee home,
I'd gladly rhyme a Summer day
   To see dear Cousin Tom.

Though parted long, my heart still clings
   To thee as to a brother;
And fancy soars on rapture's wings
   To days we spent together.

Between us rolls the ocean blue,
　　A far off home is thine ;
And new friends are not half so true
　　As those I loved langsyne.

And in that boasted land of gold,
　　Beneath a sunny sky,
You, too, may miss the friends of old
　　And merry days gone by.
And memory, roaming o'er the deep,
　　In lonely hours will turn
Back to the cloven Eildon's steep
　　And banks o' Bowden Burn.

There is one feeling of the heart
　　Where'er the footsteps roam,—
Though seas divide and long years part
　　The exile from his home,—
The memory of our place of birth
　　And youth's unclouded morn ;—
The dearest spot of all the earth,
　　That spot where we were born.

There's many weary changes there :—
   The old have passed away,
The stout back's bent with toil and care,
   The golden hair turned grey.
And in the churchyard, where we played
   Beneath the old plane tree,
The loved and dear at rest are laid
   Since you went o'er the sea.

Farewell! we both are growing old
   And ne'er may meet again ;—
That weary weary lust of gold!
   That dark and trackless main!
But could I hope this simple lay
   Had power to win thee home,
I'd gladly rhyme a Summer day
   To see dear Cousin Tom.

Bess o' Broomylea.

———

I've wandered in the mirkest night
  O'er moor and mountain grey,
When no' a starnie lent its light
  To cheer my lonely way.
Through mossy bog and meadow brook
  I've waded to the knee,
And a' to gain a'e loving look
  Fráe Bess o' Broomylea.

Oh love will light the darkest way,
  Mak' short the langsome miles,
And lift us up the steyest brae,
  And o'er the plantin' styles.

For a'e kiss o' her balmy mou',
　　A'e kind blink o' her e'e,
I wad ha'e roamed the warld through,-
　　Dear Bess o' Broomylea.

My heart wi' love loups up and down,
　　My joy I canna hide ;
I wadna' tak' a gowden crown
　　To tine my promised bride.
O' warld's gear I've little pairt,
　　But dearer far to me.
The love o' a'e fond faithfu' heart—
　　My Bess o' Broomylea.

Molly M'Shane.

Molly M'Shane will you listen to me,
Come to the window, Acushla Machree;
The tempest is howling, I'm drenched wid the rain,
But my heart is like tinder for Molly M'Shane.

Like a ghost I have stol'n from my oun cabin door,
And crossed over meadow and mountain and moor,
And here till the grey light of morn I'll remain,
For one glance of thy bright eyes, sweet Molly M'Shane.

I know I'm a fool to be loving you so,
When you've never a kind look nor word to bestow;
'Tis the spell of your beauty at work in my brain
Leads my steps to the cabin of Molly M'Shane.

Bad luck to the day that I went to the fair,—
I only saw Molly, though hundreds were there,—
And my heart from that moment was bound in love's chain,
A captive to Molly, sweet Molly M'Shane.

Big Mike swore he'd break every bone in my skin
If I looked at the road that his Molly was in,
But I left the big bouncer a howling wid pain,
And would thrash twenty more for sweet Molly M'Shane.

Sure there's love in my heart that will never expire,
There's strength in my arm that no labour can tire;
I'll toil like a baste, in a ditch or a drain,
And give all the money to Molly M'Shane.

How can you be cruel, how can you be coy,
My heart's dearest jewel, my pride and my joy!
Come shew me your face through that hole in the pane,
And give me one smile, purty Molly M'Shane.

Good luck to you now, its your face that I see,
The light of your eyes is like sunshine to me!
Contented I'll go to my cabin again,
And drame till the morning of Molly M'Shane.

Willie lo'es me weel.

Now laddie, a' your winnin' airt
  Will hae nae sway wi' me,
Ye needna seek to win my heart,—
  Its no my ain to gi'e.
For there is ane I dearly lo'e,
  A laddie kind and leal,
I ken that he will aye be true,—
  For Willie lo'es me weel.

My Mither still may scauld and ban,
  And a' the men misca',.
She says they're flatterers ilka ane,
  And Willie warst o' a.

My laddie's heart she canna ken,
　　Sae out at e'en I'll steal,
And meet him in yon bonny glen,
　　For Willie lo'es me weel.

We've climb'd Glenburnie's bonny braes,
　　Twa happy hearted bairns ;
We've den'd a'neath the blooming slaes,
　　And row'd amang the ferns.
There's mony a weary change sin' then,
　　But Willie's constant still,
And we'll be wed when Winter's gane,
　　For Willie lo'es me weel.

The Nameless Laddie.

Be kind to the bairnie that stands at the door,
The laddie is hameless and friendless and poor;
There's few hearts to pity the wee cowerin' form
That seeks at your hallin a bield frae the storm.
Your hame may be humble, your haddin' but bare,
For the lowly and poor ha'e but little to spare,
But you'll ne'er miss a morsel, though sma' be your store,
To the wee friendless laddie that stands at the door.

When the cauld blast is soughin' sae eerie and chill,
And the snaw drifts o' Winter lie white on the hill,
When ye meet in the gloamin' around the hearthstane,
Be thankfu' for haddins and hames o' your ain;

And think what the feckless and friendless maun dree,
Wi' nae heart to pity, and nae hand to gie;
That wee guileless bosom might freeze to the core
Gin ye turned the bit laddie awa frae the door.

The bird seeks a hame o'er the wide ocean wave;
In the depth o' the covert the fox has a cave;
And the hare has a den 'neath the wild winter's snaw;
But the wee dowie laddie has nae hame ava'.
Then pity the bairnie, sae feckless and lone—
Ilka gift to the poor is recorded aboon—
For the warm heart o' kindness there's blessings in store,
Sae be kind to the bairnie that stands at the door.

The Lass o' Lynwood Mill.

'Tis sweet to see the gloamin' grey
   Creep o'er the grassy fell,
And mark the sunbeams gowden ray
   Light up old Hardie's Hill :
While blossoms gay on ilka brae
   Their balmy sweets distill ;—
But ne'er a flower in glen or bower
   Like Jean o' Lynwood Mill.

Yon foplin' braw, in gilded ha',
   Wi' a' his flauntin' pride,—
Wi' artfu' tale, and studied smile,
   May woo his tinsel'd bride !

But I'll gi'e him his gilded ha',—
  I trow he's little skill,—
He disna' ken yon bonny glen,
  And Jean o' Lynwood Mill.

When rings the Auld Kirk bell we meet
  Upon yon gow'ny green !
The bonny moon looks sweetly doon
  Upon me and my Jean.
While fashion'd fair and wardly gear
  May charm wha'e'er they will !
Gi'e me my ain, my bonny Jean,—
  The lass o' Lynwood Mill.

Calum Glen.

———

Calum Glen, the bower's forsaken,
    And the trystin' hour gane by,—
No' a sound amang the bracken
    But the muircock's eerie cry.
A' the day fu' blithe and cheerie,
    I gaed linkin' but and ben!
Now my heart is sad and eerie,
    Waiting for thee, Calum Glen.

There's the little burnie sighin'
    By the cosie bracken bed,—
There's the spot where we were lyin'
    Rowed within your tartan plaid!

Ye said my lips were sweet and sappy—
   Gi'ed me kisses nine or ten,—
Simple maid was ne'er sae happy,—
   Faithless, faithless Calum Glen.

Calum Glen, the night is dark'ning,
   A' around is sad and still!—
Whisht! I hear his doggie barkin',—
   Yon's his bonnet on the hill.
Row me in your tartan plaidie!
   Kiss me, Calum, o'er again,—
There's my hand, my Highland Laddie,-
   Mak' me Mistress Calum Glen.

Cousin Nell.

Cousin Nell was a bright little thing,
　　Some seven short years ago ;
Her hair was dark as the raven's wing,
　　And her brow like the mountain snow.
Light as the sunbeams that dance on the fell
　　Was the fairy form of our Cousin Nell.

She came in the pleasant Summer time,
　　With the flowers and the honey bee ;—
Well I remember the gladsome time,
　　For she filled our home with glee.
Nothing but mirth and joy could dwell,
　　Along with our dear little Cousin Nell.

There was a blank at our cottage hearth
  When our Cousin went away!
Gone was the song and the sound of mirth
  That had cheered us many a day!
Sad were our hearts as we sighed farewell,—
  And blessings went with our Cousin Nell.

We never have seen her face again
  Since she left our Border home!
But Heaven keep her within His care
  Wherever her footsteps roam!
Enshrined in our hearts, like gladsome spell,
  Is the fairy form of our Cousin Nell.

On Reading Poems and Songs by J. G. Smith, Ednam.

O' Bard of bonny Eden side,
    Your sweet and hamely lays
Ha'e wauken'd thoughts I canna' hide,—
    Sweet thoughts o' bygane days.
Fra'e end to end I've read your buik,
    And memory's flowing free,—
The smile yet lingers on my cheek,
    The warm tear in my e'e.

To melt and thrill the bosom's chords,
    Ye've sure some witching wile ;
My lips are murmuring now the words—
    O' " Bonny Mary Lyle !"

In ilk "Farm House," the "Beggar Man,"
  A welcome guest will be,—
And a' folk bless "Wee Mary Ann,"
  And love thy "Rosalee."

Fareweel! your airtless lays will cheer
  The hearts o' auld and young,—
For what's sae sweet to Scottish ear
  As the auld mither tongue.
And should ye come to our "Town end,"
  There's hearts, baith kind and leal,
That fain wad tak' ye by the hand
  And tell ye a' they feel.

An Old Man's Song.

Sit down by me, my Guid Auld Wife,
  My kind and trusty dame,—
For ye ha'e bless'd a toil-spent life,
  And cheer'd a lonely hame.
And bring the bottle frae the bink,
  And fill wi' furthy glee
A reamin' cup, that I may drink
  A Blythe New Year to thee.

We've borne thegither Fortune's frown,—
  We seldom saw her smile,—
And strong maun be the love that's grown
  Through twa score years o' toil.

Your hair is like the Winter's snaw,
    The gloss is aff your brow,—
Auld carl Time has laid his paw
    Fu' heavy on your pow.

My heart grows grit, my guid auld May,
    And fu' o' love and pride,—
Ye're dearer now than on the day
    I brought ye hame my bride.
Then bring the bottle frae the bink,
    And fill wi' furthy glee
A reamin' cup, that I may drink
    A Guid New Year to thee.

Mary Gray.

I fain would sing a song to thee,—
  My peerless Mary Gray !
If the Muses would be kind to me,
  And tell me what to say.
If they would find some emblem meet
  For one so fair and young—
Some blossom, like thy face so sweet,
  That Bard has never sung.

But every flower that drinks the dew
  The Summer braes among,
With streaks of sunshine, skies of blue,
  Are woven into song.

The little stars that brightly gleam
  Are riven from the sky ;
The fairest of the train must beam
  Within some lady's eye.

Why should I call the daisy meek,
  Or pluck the blushing rose—
A fairer bloom's upon thy cheek
  Than any flower that blows.
While seraphs, sylphs, and angels bright
  To other climes belong,—
Such visions never met my sight,
  And shall not grace my song.

So I must try some other strain,
  Or throw my lyre by,
Since only common things remain
  In ocean, earth, or sky.
It is the beauty of the mind
  That lends so sweet a ray,
And makes thee first of womankind,
  And peerless, Mary Gray.

A Guid New Year.

Dance lightly round, ye merry hours,
   Like bairnies at their play;
We'll pu' the rose frae pleasure's bowers,
   And fling the thorns away.
Let surly Winter drive alang
   His blasts o' rain and snaw—
Be this the burden o' our sang—
   A Guid New Year to a'.
     A Guid New Year, a blythe New Year,
       In cottage and in ha',
     And routh o' joys, the hearts to cheer,
       O' lads and lasses braw

Frae Beltine tide to blythe Yule e'en,
　　Through foul and fair we toil;
But blinks o' sunshine fa' between
　　To cheer us wi' their smile.
When social mirth and friendship meet,
　　Wi' feelings fresh and young,
In ilka heart there's wishes sweet,
　　And blessing on the tongue.
　　　　　　A Guid New Year, &c.

The smile shall grace the brow of youth,
　　And every heart be gay;
While firm in friendship, love, and truth,
　　We travel life's highway.
For every friend a welcome kind;
　　For friendless forms a tear;
May blessings fa' on great and sma'
　　Throughout the coming year.
　　　　　　A Guid New Year, &c.

Scotland aye was Free.

O breathes there ane that disna lo'e
  His country and his hame!
Is there a Scottish heart that's true
  Wad change auld Scotland's name?
When first the Rose and Thistle twined,
  The tear filled mony an e'e;
And sages auld her doom foretauld,—
  For Scotland aye was a free.

Ours was a land—a free fair land,—
  Ere England had a name;
And minstrels' harp and warrior's brand
  Have aye upheld her fame.

The first in arms, in art, and song,
   She aye has borne the gree;
There's ne'er a land like Scotland yet—
   For Scotland aye was free.

On battle field and ocean wave
   Her doughty sons ha'e bled;
While History writes above their grave,
   " Here slumbers England's dead."
But the dead will sleep as calmly on
   'Neath battle, turf, or sea;—
What may they reck whose task is done—
   And Scotland still is free.

Calm Fa's the Moonbeams.

O calm fa's the moonbeams on Teviot's bright waters,
　And sweetly the starnies a' blink through the blue,—
The bonny wee flowers fauld their leaves in the gloamin',
　A' glistenin' wi' bells o' the clear silver dew.
But it isna' the moonbeams that woo me to wander,—
　It isna' the flow'rets, though bonny they be,—
But the young bloom o' beauty,—my ain winsome lassie,-
　Wha comes to her tryst by the auld willow tree.

The flowers o' the valley may blossom and wither,
　The leaves o' the forest may fa' frae the tree,
The roses may fade on the cheek o' my lassie,
　And time dim the light o' her bonny black e'e.
But leal love will last though beauty may wither,—
　And faithfu' to Jeanie I aye will remain,—
For the charms o' the mind are the ties which endure aye,
　And bind me to love her when beauty is gane.

The Wee Sweep Laddie.

A gruesome auld carle ance cam' to our door,
  Wi' a bairnie baith barefit an' duddie,—
A' barkened an' blackened wi' mony a score
  Was the face o' the Wee Sweep Laddie.

We were fash'd wi' the reek, and the lum was to clean ;
  Sae a bargain was made wi' his daddie ;
But little we thocht that the carle's machine
  Wad turn out—the Wee Sweep Laddie.

His wee heart was fu', and the saut tears ran,—
  It was waefu' to hear his bit greetie,—
As up the dark lum at the carle's comman',
  He clam' wi' his wee black feetie.

Syne a farle a cake frae my grannie he got ;
    And she ca'ed him a brave little mannie ;—
How happy he looked when a new silver groat
    Shone bright in his wee black han'ie.

Sax towmonds were gane, when a braw strappin' lad,
    Cam' to our door buskit fu' guady,—
We scarce could believe our ain e'en, when he said
    That he ance was the Wee Sweep Laddie.

Oh waefu' and sad was the tale he did tell ;
    How that he had been stoun frae his daddie,—
An' o' a' the suffering and toil that befell
    When he was a Wee Sweep Laddie.

And often we speak o' the wee barefit chiel,
    Wi' the cowl and the auld sooty plaidie,—
And ban' at the gruesome auld carle that could steal
    Awa' frae his hame a bit laddie.

Weary Winter.

Oh dowie, dowie, is the heart
   In the Winter o' the year,—
Nae gay green leaf to glad the sight,
   Nae sunny blink to cheer.
But the norlan' wind comes laden,
   Wi' bitin' frost an' snaw!
Oh weary, weary Winter!
   I wish ye were awa'.

We hae a hame, a cosie hame,—
   And thankfu' may we be,—
For nae bield has the cowerin bird,
   When the leaf is aff the tree ;—

And wee, wee barefit bairns hae left
  Their fit-prints in the snaw !
Oh weary, weary Winter,
  I wish ye were awa.

Come lo'esome Spring, wi' a your braws,
  To cleed the hill and lea,—
And bring the blue back'd swallow,
  Frae o'er the briny sea.
Sweet hope will nestle in the heart,
  When sunny blossoms blaw ;
And weary, weary Winter
  Will soon be far awa'.

A Winter Night.

Gae steek the shutters on the blast,
   Keep out the drivin' snaw ;
And thankfu' be this night we're safe
   Within a bigit wa'.
The ragin' storm, that rocks the roof,
   And dirls our cottage door,
May on some houseless wanderer beat
   Upon the lonely moor.

The shepherd he maun brave the blast,
   To seek his sheep a biel' ;
Nae comrade but the faithfu' dog,
   That shivers at his heel.

O'er weary wastes, he wanders wide,
　　Far, far frae hut or ha',—
And finds a grave on lonely height,
　　'Aneath a wreath o' snaw !

The heart that's hapit, bien, and warm,—
　　Wi' bearin' proud an' bauld,—
Thinks little o' the friendless form
　　Maun thole the Winter's cauld.
But there are hames wi' fireless hearths,
　　Where breadless bairnies cower !
Ah ! little kens the rich and great
　　The sufferings o' the poor.

O weels me on the open ear,
　　Will list' a tale o' woe,—
And on the warm and loving heart
　　Whence streams o' kindness flow.
How sound and sweet their sleep will be,
　　Amid the Winter's storm,
Wha wipes the tear frae poortith's e'e,
　　And shields the houseless form.

To the Memory of the Ettrick Shepherd.

Beside the lone St Mary,
　　They have raised to him a pile,—
'Mid the haunts of elf and fairy,
　　The scenes he loved so well.
And though the frame be perished,
　　And clay be turned to clay,—
His memory still is cherished,
　　And the stain is wiped away.

The wild flowers of the mountain,
　　Around his brow entwine,—
Bring blossoms from the fountain
　　To grace thy Poet's shrine.

The skylark from the heather
　Will rise and sing his fame,—
And his matin hymn for ever
　Be vocal with his name.

The Rifle Volunteers.

———

Yon Eagle with the brooding brow
   Would soar across the main,—
His pinions, plucked at Waterloo,
   Have gathered strength again.
He deems, within his place of pride,
   To wear the British Crown,—
To pluck fair England's Rose, and tread
   Our bearded Thistle down.

Fair Albion saw the coming storm,—
   Her banner broad appears,—
She gave the gathering cry—to form
   Her Rifle Volunteers.

With heart of steel and willing hand,
  For merry England's law,—
Yon brooding Eagle still must bend
  Beneath the Lion's paw.

Auld Scotland heard the bodin' soun',
  And threw her crook away !
Now, foul fa' ilka coward loon,
  Wha winna join the fray !—
Syne banged her gun frae aff the wa',
  Wi' belt and bayonet keen,
And swore to conquer or to fa',
  To keep her Thistle green.

There's ae auld toun by Teviot's side,
  That's famed in days o' yore,—
Her independence is her pride,
  And loyal to the core.
There's ae auld flag maun waive on high,
  When Scotland's foe appears,—
And " Teribus," the battle cry
  O Hawick Volunteers.

Langsyne.

A wee bit name, but sweet's the sound,
  And saft, saft is the spell,—
And dear to memory is the tale,
  The simple words can tell.
For fondly still the heart will cling,
  And thought and feeling twine,
Round bygane days, and ilka thing,
  That breaths o' Auld Langsyne.

Oh blissfu' vision—now I see
  My ain auld hame again,—
Wi' mony a face o' lauchin' glee,
  Around the auld hearthstane.

Twa gentle e'en, wi' love's ain beam,—
 A little hand in mine !—
Be still, my heart—it's but a dream—
 A vision o' Langsyne.

The glossy brow is careworn now,
 The gowden hair is grey ;
Auld hearts, that aye were kind and true,
 Are mingling with the clay !
A silent hame,'a cauld, cauld hearth,
 A sad and broken shrine ;—
I hear nae mair the voice o' mirth,
 ・That rang sae sweet Langsyne.

Oh ruthless Time, what joys are gane,—
 The dearest and the best !
What gowden dreams a' dream'd in vain,
 Lie buried in the past.
We've mony a cherished hope to mourn,—
 Yet why should age repine,—
For " Thoughts that breathe, and words that
 Still hallow Auld Langsyne.

The Auld Smiddy End.

O the Auld Smiddy end, where in youth's happy day
A merry band o' bairnies wad gather at their play ;
I mind the happy faces, and the hours we wad spend
Wi' the bools and the peeries, at the Auld Smiddy end.

Against the battered gabel, were mony ora things—
Auld pleughs that wanted couters ; new wheels that wanted
      rings ;
A pair o' broken harrows, that for years had lain to mend ;—
There was meikle claithin' riven at the Auld Smiddy end.

O the fun and frolic, and the mischief that we wrought,—
There was lums to set alow, and battles to be fought,—
And jury courts to haud when some coward laddie hen'd,-
And gat his buttons scartit at the Auld Smiddy end.

We never thought o' partin' at the hour o' gloamin' grey,
The fun was aye beginnin' when the daylight was away ;
When bedin' time cam' round, ilka mither brawly ken'd
She wad find her truant laddie at the Auld Smiddy end.

And in Winter we wad gather round the bleesin' smiddy
    hearth,—
While block and stithy rang wi' our daffin' an' our mirth ;
The independent blacksmith—to kings he wadna bend—
Was kind to the laddies at the Auld Smiddy end.

But youthfu' pleasures winna' last, and youthfu' scenes will
    change ;—
The smiddy and the smith are gane, and ilka thing is
    strange ;—
'Mang a' the happy faces,that in ither days I ken'd,
There's nane to meet me noo at the Auld Smiddy end.

But in the quiet gloamin' hour I sit and muse alane,
Till Fancy, wi' her fairy wand, brings vanished scenes again ;
The Memory, like a bird, to its ain hame will wend,
And familiar faces gather round the Auld Smiddy end.

Mary's Grave.

———

The quiet dead are round me,—
   The mourners all are gone,—
And evening's shade has found me,
   Beside thy grave, alone.
Thy name I have not spoken,
   Since thou breathed thy maiden vow!
But death the tie has broken ;—
   I may speak of thee now.

So young, so fair, yet faithless !—
   Last year a willing bride !
And dearer, cold and breathless,
   Than all the world beside.

Where is thy chosen lover,
 That he kneels not by my side?
He left thee for another,—
 And of broken vows thou died!

Ev'ry earthly tie must sever.
 Again I cross the wave!
Farewell my home, for ever,—
 My Mary 's in the grave!

The Muirland Maid.

" Gin ye will leave your muirland hame,
   An' kin o' low degree,
To wed wi' ane o' noble name,—
   Wi' rank an' wealth to gie !
A coronet shall grace thy brow,.
   Rich diamonds deck thy hair,—
And gallants gay before thee bow—
   The fairest o' the fair !"

' Though humble be my muirland hame,
   My kin o' low degree,—
Though mine be but a peasant's name,
   I winna' wed wi' thee.

I couldna thole your Sister's spite,
　　Your Mither's haughty pride,—
Sae ye maun turn your steed, Sir Knight,
　　An' seek some richer bride."

" Now, by the rose upon thy cheek,
　　The love light o' thine e'e,—
Nae richer bride I'll ever seek,
　　Gin ye will wed wi' me.
My Sister's spite, my Mother's pride,
　　Ye'll ha'e nae cause to fear,—
For they will gie my bonny bride,
　　A welcome kind and dear."

" Sir Knight, your words are soft and kind,
　　Could I believe them true
I'd leave my muirland hame behind,
　　An' gang alang wi' you."
" Then gie to me your lily hand ;—
　　I'll aye be true to thee !—
The fairest maid in broad Scotland,
　　This night my bride shall be ! "

John Barleycorn.

————

Fareweel, John Barleycorn, fareweel
   Nae mair your scorn I'll dree ;
I ha'e been dancin' to the deil
   Through love o' barley bree.
But I will bear nae mair the badge,
   That I sae lang ha'e borne ;—
For there's my hand, I'll sign the pledge !—
   Fareweel, John Barleycorn !

On Hogmanay some friends I met,—
   We set us blith'ly down,—
An' mirth and fun and flaughts o' wit,
   Were flashin' roun' an' roun'.

An' aye we ca'd the ither coag,
  An' toom'd the reamin' horn!
O but ye be a wylin' rogue,—
  Fareweel, John Barleycorn!

A happier core was never met,
  There ne'er was better cheer;
Wi' jugs o' toddy reekin' het,
  We hail'd the comin' year.
Our arms grew sair wi' shakin' hands,—
  We a' were brithers sworn,—
Sae firm and fast were friendships bands
  Tied o'er John Barleycorn.

But whiles a wee bit spark o' light
  Will raise an unco' low;
An' bicker bands, though e'er sae tight,
  Are easy broken through.
Ae jarrin' word raised sic' a fray,
  That friendships links were torn;
An' supple neives began to play—
  Fareweel, John Barleycorn!

I tried my best to redd the row,—
    Up to my feet I sprang;
But got a cloit upon the pow,
    That nearly spoil'd my sang.
Ye've been the cause o' muckle wae,
    O meikle scaith and scorn;
I'll sign the pledge this very day!
    Fareweel, John Barleycorn!

Lines by R. Menon, Dunbar, on Reading Widow's Lament.

———

Dear Sir, though we be far apart,—
I feel a throbbin' at my heart
    O' telegraphic fire,
That urges me to gang to wark,
An' frae the muse draw out a spark
    To flash alang the wire.

But I confess I'm at a loss,
My fancies wander, turn and toss,
    To ken what I should say.
To write to ane I dinna' ken,
Tak's a' the ink out o' the pen,—
    It seems to shrink away.

I kenna if you're young or auld,
Or if you're head be grey or bald ;
  But I can plainly see,
By yon sad dirge ye wrote sae weel,
That ye ha'e got a heart to feel,—
  An' that's enough for me.

The Widow's grief, sae deep and keen,
Was far ower sacred to be seen,
  An' wanted nane to scan.
Perhaps it reach'd the Spirit's ear,—
Though what she said nae mair could hear
  Her care relieved Guidman.

Few can imagine—nane express—
The crushin' weight o' that distress
  That preys upon the heart
O them who've lived a Christian life
For forty years as man an' wife,—
  When death says you maun part.

Yes—theirs is love deserves the name—
A chasten'd, pure and holy flame,—
  Such love as Angels share :

Unlike that flame fond youth inspires,
Blawn up an' fed by fierce desires,—
    Dies out and warms nae mair.

I've view'd the case, and maun confess
Oft breath'd a wish o' selfishness
    I first might tak' the road ;—
But love an' pity for each other
Suggests, we baith should gang together,
    If 'twere the will o' God.

Dear Sir, accept, and kind excuse,
Those humble breathings o' my muse,
    As thanks for what you sent.
Such gifts as these—I often think—
Got up wi' paper, pen an' ink,
    Are friendship's best cement.

Dreamings of Home.

When the heart grows sick of the cares of life,
  And sear'd with the world's scorn,
The memory will turn to our youthful days,
  And the spot where we were born :

And visions bright of that happy time
  Come floating upon the brain,
As on fancy's wings we are borne away
  To the home of our youth again.

I dream of an old and shadowy wood,
  Green bowers, and a mossy seat;
Of a wild bird's song, of a murmuring stream,
  And flowers beneath my feet.

I have mingled in the world's strife,
    And tasted its hopes and fears ;
And I'm far away from the friends I love,
    And the home of my happy years.

I have found that pleasure has passed with youth,
    And sorrow with age has come ;
But I still love to dwell on the scenes of the past,
    And dream of my native home.

Spring.

The Winter sat lang on muirland and fell,—
Wee lammies lay deein' on ilka hill,—
And the herdsmen's hearts grew dowie and sad
At the wearyfu' wark Jock Frost had made.

But the Spring peep'd in wi' her lauchin' e'e,
And opened the blossom's on hill and lea ;
The birds o' the Simmer came o'er the faem,
And twittered fu' blythe in their ain auld hame.

Then the e'e grew bright that was dim wi' wae,
The heart grew young, though the hair was grey,
When Auld Mither Earth, in her joy and pride,
Arrayed hersel' like a brisk young bride.

We winna misca' the Winter's reign,

For ilka season has joys o' her ain ;

But when skies are blue and birds sing clear,

We canna but lo'e the Spring o' the year.

The Lassie that ye Lo'e.

'Tis sweet in lightsome Simmer days,
   When flowers are a' in bloom,
To wander 'mang the bonny braes
   Where grows the whin and broom.

But Nature's joys ha'e nae the power
   To make the bosom glow
And cheer the heart like ae sweet hour
   Wi' the Lassie that ye lo'e.

When gloamin' gathers o'er the scene,
   And Phœbus steeks his e'e,
And ye maun meet your Kate or Jean
   'Aneath the trystin' tree—

The blushing cheek will tell love's tale—
   When hearts are leal and true—
And brawly can ye read love's smile
   In the Lassie that ye lo'e.

The Fisher's Song.

The laverock frae the fleecy clud
  Pours out his early sang—
The sillar saughs are in the bud,
  As down the glen we gang ;—
As down the buskit glen we gang,
  The green grass to our knee ;
While beads o' dew like diamonds hang
  In clusters frae the tree.
        Then gi'e to me my rod and reel,
          Wi' drake and woodcock flee ;
        And I maun ha'e the fisher's creel—
          The water side for me.

The merry birds in bower and dell
  Ha'e wauken'd frae their dream ;
The cowslip lifts its yellow bell
  To meet the sun's first beam.
And ilka sound's a sound of mirth,
  Frae streamlet, sky, and tree;
There 's no' in a' the wide, wide earth,
  A sweeter scene can be.
      Then gi'e to me, &c.

Now, here's the spot to cast the flee,
  Below the dimpled linn ;
The trouts are rising fast and free,
  And dart on quiverin' fin.
There 's music in the soughin' wand,
  And in the whirrin' reel,
As we bring them dancing to the strand,
  And stow them in the creel.
      Then gi'e to me, &c.

And when the sun aboon our head
  Shines wi' a fiercer beam,
We'll seek the cooling plantin' shade,
  And set us down to dream ;—

To dream awa' an idle hour
 Amang the leaves sae green,
And trow the world an Eden bower
 Where sin has never been.
   Then gi'e to me, &c.

Wha wadna leave the dinsome Toun,
 Wi' a' its strife and noise,
To hear the pleasant water's soun',
 And share the fisher's joys !
There 's pleasure o'er a social gill,
 Wi' cronies frank and free ;
But the rod and reel, the fisher's creel,
 The water side for me !
   Then gi'e to me, &c.

Address to the Brethren of St James' Lodge—(424).

Sons of Light around me shining,—
  'Neath the great Omnicient Eye,—
Friendship, Love, and Truth combining,
  Bind us in their rosy tie ;—
Bind us by each sign and token,—
  By each hieroglyphic dear,—
By the Word, that's never spoken
  Save in Fellow Craftsman's ear.

Steadfast in the paths of duty,
  Rugged Ashlers yet shall rise,—
Piles of Wisdom, Strength and Beauty,
  'Neath our bright and silver skies.

Fear not ;—Masonry shall flourish,
Spite of Pope or Layman's ban,
While the laws of Love we cherish—
Peace on earth—Good will to man !

The Faded Flower.

———

There's joy in every woodland bower,
    Where happy birds are singing,—
And mirth around each cottage door,
    Where childhood's laugh is ringing!
But there's nae joy at our hearthstane,
    Nae happy faces gathered,—
A' sighing for a flower that's gane,—
    A little blossom withered.

We watched our darling day by day,
    Upon her pillow lying,—
We saw the roses fade away,
    And knew that she was dying.

Yet she grew sweeter as she dwined,
    And dearer to our bosom,—
Our heart strings close and closer twined
    Around our little blossom!

'Twas morning—and the sunshine free
    Was through the lattice falling,—
The birds sang on the apple tree,
    Like Angel voices calling!
The last sigh heaved her gentle breast,—
    Our last fond kiss was given!
Her sinless spirit joined the blest,—
    And sought a home in Heaven!

In Memoriam.

Go scatter o'er that lowly bed,
   The blossoms sweet and wild,—
And place a white rose at his head,—
   Type of that sainted child;
For sweeter blossom ne'er had bloom,
Than he who lies within the tomb!

Sad was his fate,—he left our hearth
   A happy hearted boy,
His silvery voice rang gaily forth
   In melody and joy,—
And ere the echo ceased to play
His stainless soul had passed away!

The beaming eye is beamless now
That shed so soft a ray,—
The curls that clustered round his brow
Are mouldering in the clay ;—
But, in a happier abode,
His gentle soul is with his God !

O'er the Moor amang the Heather.
(NEW VERSION.)

Oh love has wrought me meikle ill ;
    And drink has played me mony a pliskie ;
And guid befriend the luckless chiel
    That's led astray by love and whiskie !
A Hawick gill was in my e'e,—
    My heart as light as ony feather,—
When, warm wi' love and barley bree,
    I cross'd the moor amang the heather.

        O'er the moor amang the heather,
        O'er the moor amang the heather ;
        Blooming braes in Summer days
        Are rugged roads in Wintry weather.

When deevels drive, ane needs maun rin ;
   And sae I ran to Maggie Miller ;
The wit was out, the drink was in,—
   I wadna stayed awa' for siller.
The road was rough, and lang the way,
   And lowering cluds began to gather ;
And six lang miles 'atween us lay
   Out o'er the moor amang the heather.

The gurly wind wi' ragin' thuds
   Was like to rive my claes in taters ;
And frae the dark and drumlie cluds,
   The rain blast rushed in angry blatters.
My hazel staff I gripit fast,
   My hat upon my head did tether ;
And, careless o' the drivin' blast,
   I crossed the moor amang the heather.

Across the bents I lightly strode,
   And skiped o'er ilk knowe and craggie ;
I thought nae on the langsome road,
   I only thought on bonny Maggie.

The moon—that whiles had lent her light—
   Now closed her lantern a'thegether;
And mid the darkness o' the night
   I tint the path amang the heather.

At times I stood, at times I ran,
   And floundered o'er the bogs and ditches;
And whiles a wee bit prayer began,
   To fley awa' the ghaists and witches.
Without the bield o' bush or tree
   To screen me frae the Wintry weather,
I thought to lay me down and dee,
   Upon the moor amang the heather.

What eerie thoughts ran through my mind,—
   I sighed a last fareweel to Maggie!
And wondered wha my bouk wad find,
   Deep laired within some mossy haggie.
At last I spied a spark o' light,
   Like a wee star in Heaven glowing;
'Twas Maggie's cruzie, flaming bright
   Its beams across the muirland throwing.

Oh kindly words are sweet to hear,—

    And love's fond tale is past revealing,—

And sweet the sympathetic tear,

    Down rosy cheek like dew drap stealing.

Beside her ingle, bleesin' bright,—

    Loof locked in loof—we sat together;

And I forgot that dreary night,

    Upon the moor amang the heather.

        O'er the moor amang the heather,

        O'er the moor amang the heather;

        Blooming braes in Summer days

        Are rugged roads in Wintry weather.

The Tocherless Lassie.

Leese me on the day when the Laird o' Blawearie
  On his auld Highland pownie rode up to our door;
I sat by the ingle cheek, dowie an' eerie,
  A tocherless Lassie, baith friendless an' poor.

My Faither was laird o' a weel stockit mailin;
  He had kye in the haugh, he had sheep on the hill;
But the puir simple bodie, he lost ilka shillin',
  An' brought us to poortith by signin' a bill.

I had wooers nae few when the sillar was plenty,
  An' ilka ane vow'd for my love he wad dee;
But they soon fled awa' when the gear it grew scanty,
  An' left me to mourn wi' the tear in my e'e.

I kenn'd that my beauty wad soon be a' fadin',—
  Though my cheek was yet rosy, an' white was my
    brow,—
An' I thought I was ettled to dee an auld maiden,
  When luck sent the Laird o' Blawearie to woo.

The Laird he was feckless, an' fash'd wi' the
    breathin' ;
  His chafts were fa'en in, an' his teeth were a' gane ;
But he proffer'd a carriage an' meiklé braw claithin,
  An' I trow'd the auld body was better than nane.

Ere a towmond had gane, I was ance mair a wanter ;
  But now I was ledy o' houses an' land ;
An' a' my braw wooers cam back in a canter,—
  An' ilka ane thought he was sure o' my hand.

Where ance I had nane, now I reckon'd a dizzen,
  An' weel did they flatter, an' sair did they strive.
The dinkit toun's dandies around me cam' bizzin',
  Like bumbees that follow the queen o' the hive.

The Priest o' the parish, the spruce young Dissenter,
 Were daily attendants at denner an' tea,—
An' oft, in the gloamin', the cripple Presenter
 Sang sweet serenades 'neath the auld apple tree.

But Jamie cam' hame—ance a herd wi' my Faither—
 I ken'd that he aye had a likin' for me ;—
When bairnies we played on the muirland thegether,
 And harried the byke o' the wild foggy bee.

Sae I gied him my hand, an' we're happy an' cheerie,
 Wi' scores o' guid sheep gae'n white on the lea.
But often I think o' the Laird o' Blawearie,
 And the day when he first cam' a wooin' to me.

Willie's on the Sea.

Oh dinna bid me join your mirth,
 For daffin' gi'es me pain ;
There 's nae a lainlier lass on earth,
 Sin' my dear laddie 's gane.
He left his native land behind,
 A sailor he wad be ;—
I hear the angry Wintry wind,—
 An' Willie 's on the sea.

He gae to me a gowden ring
 Afore he gaed awa',—
An' said he wad be back ere Spring
 Had clad the greenwood shaw.

But Spring an' Simmer baith are gane,—
    An' snaw drifts hide the lea ;—
An' yet I wander a' my lane,—
    My Willie 's on the sea.

I maunna' doubt his faithfu' heart,
    Nor think that he's to blame ;
I mind how sair it was to pairt,
    The day he left his hame.
When Winter's gane, and lightsome Spring
    Has clad our trystin' tree,—
The gentle breezes yet may bring
    My Willie frae the sea.

A Farewell to Scotland.

The boat lies at the river strand,
  The wind blaws fresh and free;
Land o' my love, my heather land,
  A last farewell to thee.
The bonny glen where gowan's grow
  Beside the lowly shiel';
The wimplin' burn, the broomy knowe,
  For ever fare-thee-weel.

They say that foreign skies are blue
  And nature's face is fair;
They say that flowers o' gaudy hue
  Breathe fragrance through the air.

But the Heather and the gowden Broom,
   The Thistle bauld and free,
Are Freedom's flowers, and winna bloom
   In lands ayont the sea.

I ne'er may tread her hills again,
   Her forests or her fells ;
I ne'er may see the bonny glen
   Where peace and beauty dwells :—
But on whatever sod I kneel
   I'll bless her honoured name,
And breathe a prayer for Scotland's weal,-
   My Country, and my Hame.

Ingram Content Group UK Ltd.
Milton Keynes UK
UKHW021959100423
419951UK00005B/120